Rain
A Poetic Memoir

by
udbhavi upadhyay

Illustrations by Dipti Ronghe

Dedicated to my Mum and all the other influential women in my life.

CONTENTS

ABOUT THE BOOK

When I was in 4th Standard, my class teacher used to really fathom the way I wrote my answers. She used to jokingly say, 'This girl will be a writer, one day. Look at the way she writes expressing what she feels about the literary piece along with the question asked. She answers in her own way!'

Time passed and I forgot all about it. My answers grew shorter and more mechanical, to keep them to the point but Mum, being a writer herself, never let me forget those words. 'This girl will be a writer, one day!' She pushed me to write about everything. About the happy trips we took; beautiful trees and mountains, the sun and the moon, my experience at school, and when life got tough and I had to choose my subjects for further studies. She pushed me to write.

Even when Mum got sick and the doctor said she might be on the brink of falling to the other side, I would write. I would write my thoughts, my vulnerabilities and my insecurities in poems. I would write my fears and my scars. How I felt when there were fights at home and I didn't know where else I could go. I wrote when I broke my leg and I was away from home. I wrote how homesick I felt every single day, and how badly I missed dancing. I wrote about everything, but I never shared it with anyone apart from my mum and my sister until 2019. This is when I was working at an events company, which invited notable people from different industries to come and speak about ideas at a huge stage. A renowned American poet was invited to mentor us on how to go about dealing with these speakers and have a dramatic effect on people. He asked us if anyone of us knew how to do poetry.

I was looking down at a pen that was lying on the floor for long. A colleague called my name out. I was startled. This colleague knew I was onto something, during the breaks, and she wanted me to come out of my closet. But I had never gathered the courage to show my diary to her or well, anyone else. As I approached the centre of the room, I was asked to share whatever I had written, lately. And with fear in my heart and a meek voice, I just read out what I had written about an infamous rape case that had recently happened in Mumbai.

When I finished reciting the piece, I got a reaction that I did not expect. Everyone had stopped working in the office and a few of my colleagues even had tears in their eyes. There was pin drop silence for a while, followed by applause for my piece. I felt like my poem reached them. I felt heard.

When the COVID-19 pandemic struck, I found myself with an abundance of time. So, I gathered all the poems I had penned and began sharing some of them on social media. Soon, people started recognizing me as a poet, and that magical feeling of recognition provided a glimmer of hope to me amidst those dark times. In the face of death's proximity, hope began to blossom within me. That single question and realization transformed me into a more confident person. It was then, my journey with writing my first book began.

I struggled with the theme of the book for long but it just struck me one day. While working on my office computer in Mumbai after the pandemic, one day, I just knew the theme of my book.

The book title 'Rain' symbolizes rebirth, foreboding, introspection, and the breaking of the drought. What does it mean to me?

Rain means love but it also means heartbreak. It makes me remember my good and bad days. Days when my soul transports me to my childhood home, my home garden, long drives, pretty little lies, and foods with strong smells. And days that made me feel like escaping to my safe space. I am reminded of how girls grow up differently than boys.

After traversing the scorching desert of self-doubt and procrastination, here comes a downpour of emotions drenched landscape of my confidence.

I extend my heartfelt gratitude to all those who have supported me on this journey and made me feel confident enough to share my poems with the world. My heartiest thanks to my friends, family, my dear mentors and readers.

Dear Readers,

As I sit here with a heart filled with gratefulness and a pen in my hand, I find it challenging to put into words, the depth of emotions that swell within me. The completion of my poetry book, 'Rain', marks the ending of a profound journey, one that I have traversed with every ounce of devotion and vulnerability in my being. And now, as you hold this book in your hands, I feel a sense of excitement, knowing that my words have found their way to you.

These poems have been my friend in times of joy and sorrow, my shelter when the world felt overwhelming, and my voice when words failed me. And now, they have taken on a life of their own.

The poems in this book are not just about me—they are about you, too. They are an invitation to introspection, a mirror that reflects sentiments we all experience as human beings. May this book become a cherished companion!

With the deepest gratitude,

Udbhavi Upadhyay
(Author)

ON A DARK NIGHT IN JUNE...

Mum screamed and shouted,
holding her tummy, so big.
Twisted and turned,
The doctor said, she was sick.

Clouds rumbled and thundered,
for years it hadn't rained.
A roar of a tiger.
There was fear
in the air.

The world stopped
and then started yet again.

After hours and hours,
of moaning and yelling.
A baby was born.
The clouds thundered her name.

– Born a girl in a patriarchal world.

POETRY COMES RUNNING TO ME...

Poetry comes running to me,
often like a child.
Hugs me by my knees tight,
with its eyes lit up like the sky
on New Year's night.

Talking gibberish to me,
in a small voice,
indulging me in its petite joys.

Maybe it wants me to reminisce
my golden days, when my heart was pure
and away from all the noise.

At that moment, my battled heart
comes to peace,
and my weary hungry soul
finds itself a feast.

Poetry comes running to me,
often like a child.

– Poetry is like a wild child full of love to give.

I WISH I WAS A CLOUD...

I wish I could be a cloud,
grand and free.
I'd travel to any place,
and be friends with the breeze.

I wish I could bring rain,
when dear humans cried out loud
on a hot summer day,
for some relief.

I wish I could be a cloud
for I'd have my own music and melodies.

I'd dance with the ocean,
flirt with the trees.

I wish I could break free.
I wish I was a cloud.

**– Thoughts I have in the middle of an
important meeting in the office.**

LOTUS IN THE MUD…

In a joint family of 25,
A new born girl opened her eyes.
The strange new world waited for her ahead,
Shocks and traumas:
king-sized.

Born and brought up,
Like a lotus in the mud.
With another sister incoming,
the child naturally did woman up.

Struggled, and hustled,
to keep a roof over our heads.
Mum was tired all the time,
Dad could not take a minute's rest.

Loved to travel,
But dreams have a price.
They're measured in money,
not how someone is 'nice'.

We'd be millionaires,
who'd go to work on a flight.
If only goodness paid,
And if the world was so kind.

Violence around us,
Debts to pay.
children kept quiet,
and Mum would pray.

Struggled through the mess,
But grew up in peace.
For Mum taught us to love,
Even when everyone deceives.

I ASKED THE DEEP BLUE NIGHT SKY

I asked the deep blue night sky,
'Why are you sad?'
He said, 'I am fine!'
And then it started to rain.
The sky can't hide its tears like Mum often does.

– Looking at the sky on a rainy night.

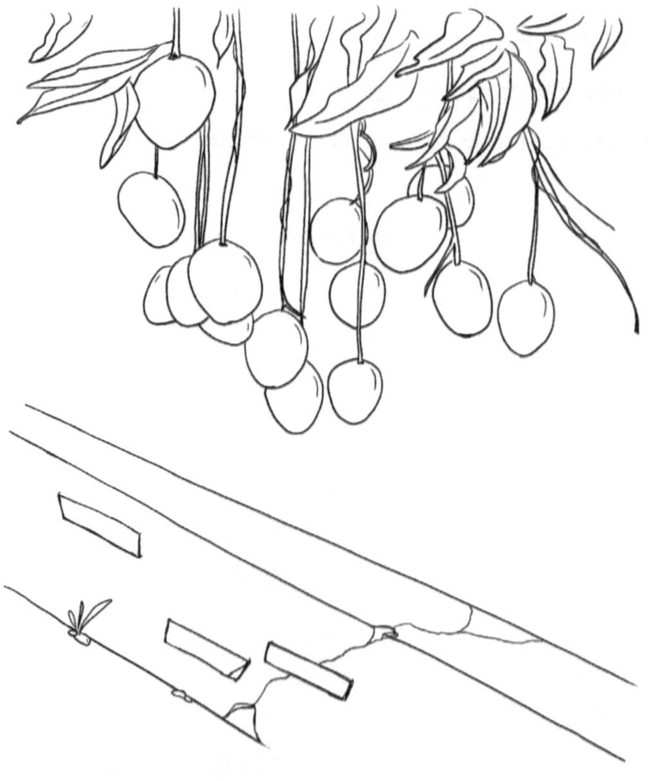

MANGO SEASON

June commenced,
and Mangoes bloomed in my lane.
It was a quiet summer night,
but then it started to rain.

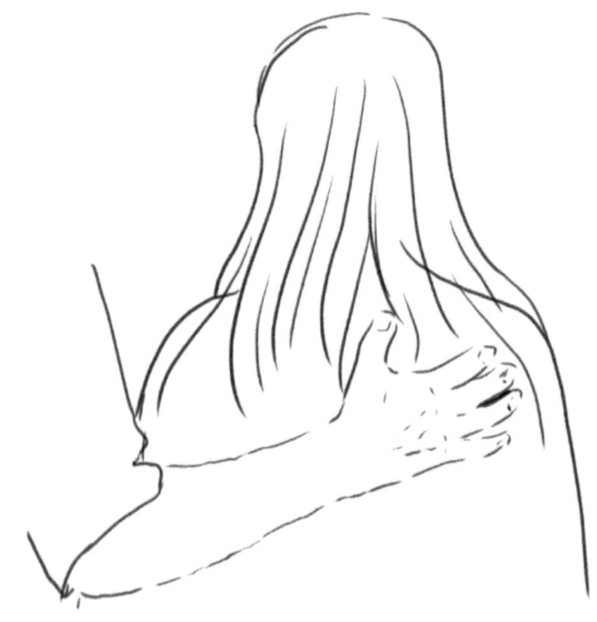

ALWAYS AROUND

There was a fight at home,
back when we were kids.
My sister had even called the police!
I had a nervous breakdown &
my mother was losing her calm.

The fight went on for hours and hours,
oh, it didn't stop.
Mum wanted to flee, Dad was troubled
& the sun was burning hot.

We didn't know what else to do,
we were young and naive.
There was some mention of banishment
and of guns and knives.

A hand touched Mum from behind,
and suddenly all her worries went to the bin.
She smiled at last with peace.
It was my long-gone grandfather's spirit
telling her to be at ease.

– Our Guardian Angel is always with us.

THE ROOM

"We had a small room where we grew up; my sister & I. It was our Paradise."

Rusty and woody,
the attic smelled.
Small like a bunker, it often felt.

A Safe Haven away from the world.
Amidst the chaos was our personal universe.

Nobody had access to it, there we could be free.
We'd build castles out of batteries,
and bump cars into trees.
I travel a lot now,
but the Room is all, where I wish to be.
No expectations from the world,
no pressure, to be.

Our room, or the attic,
is what I dearly miss.
It was our Safe Haven, our paradise!
Oh! What a bliss!

DON'T CLIP HER WINGS

"We dance for laughter, we dance for pain."

I loved dancing since I was 4,
It made me feel a whirl of joy.
It made all my worries vanish,
Beneath the vast blue sky.

I would move in motion,
With music in my brain.
I would crash and burn,
I would make the clouds rain.

Dark, came a night,
He didn't like my might.
My confidence, my power,
my beautiful life.

He came alone to my house,
Didn't speak or greet me.
Just took away, my dancing shoes,
at the first glance, from beneath me.

He took my dancing shoes away,
But, oh, not without a fight,
For I had worn them to the bone,
Dancing through endless nights.

He came and stole all my joys away,
and left me feeling sore.
He wrapped his icy grip around me,
and threatened me to the core.

I rise here, again now,
with all the inventory I have.
I will dance better than yesterday,
knowing it can get lost.

Who was he, you ask?
I dare say his name.
It was not a single person,
But a group of people
who feel shame.

Who cannot see a girl dance,
Cannot see her high,
Can just clip her wings,
when she dreams to fly.

– Let them spread their wings and fly freely.

PINK FROCK

"There was a pink frock, Mum gifted me.
Have you seen it?"

I'd wear it at Breakfast,
let it never be out of sight.
I'd wear it all day,
and even at night.

My favourite dress,
in my perfect world.
Obsessed with it,
I'd twirl and twirl.

I outgrew my dress,
and my body grew,
All my clothes turned black,
and pink dresses were now few.

I wanted new things;
Goth music and rap.
Innocence was lost,
and along came a generation gap.

That gift from Mum
made me feel like a pretty little girl.
A princess, even.
Now, I am not too sure.

My world was beautiful,
And I dreamt and prayed.
Believed in magic,
And believed people stayed.

Gone is my childhood,
I don't feel so free.
Now, I look in the mirror,
I don't like what I see.

A realist, a pessimist
Where's that wonder and joy?
Where's that girl in a pink frock,
She surrendered, why?

Where is that girl in me,
Who just wants to dance?
Who wants to enjoy every moment,
And play with ants.

There was a pink frock, Mum gifted me.
It's lost now,
Can't seem to find it,
I've been looking all around.

– Call me asap, if you find it! Okay?

THUNDERSTORM

Inexplicably strange, like in an old dream.
Bound, by the highs and lows of society.
Like tides, washing away with that cosmic force,
wind forming deforming.
Sand dunes reverse cutting through a rock
and making way.

He came in like a thunderstorm
and took my breath away.

MIRROR

"Once my professor asked me, what I missed the most from back home.
Me: My wall-sized mirror."

Nostalgia hits me, when I think about,
the giant wall-sized mirror in my Room
at my native house.

Old and worn out, beautiful and brave.
The mirror showed me possibilities,
which were always there.

It took me to places,
it made me fly.
I danced looking at it. I acted, I cried.

He was my friend, my only escape.
I hadn't found writing yet, I was not of age.

I'd become a princess looking at it,
or be the Lady of the Lake.
I would talk to it when I needed a friend.

A sinking little feeling,
I have inside;
If I can ever look in that mirror,
with hope in my eyes.

Somehow that mirror
still comes in my dreams.
Where my Mum watches me dance,
and I still believe.

That I have a magic portal,
embedded in my head.
To dream is to live,
it isn't naive.

SCHOOL

"My school's castle is the most beautiful building, I have ever seen. Or maybe not. It is just very damn special."

We were growing up, all right.

Everyone was aware.

Up all night, with not a single care.

A beautiful time, a beautiful place.

With some beautiful friends,

we'd dominate the stairs.

Changing bodies, gaining weight.
Puberty hit us right,
childhood jumped off the front gate.

Low-waist skirts, teachers on alert.
Late-night texts, and group bunks.

Stupid games, and watching Mean Girls.
Winning trophies, going for States.
Monitoring class, and performing on stage.
Breaking hearts but getting good grades.

Attractions and crushes,
heartbreaks and pain.
Excitement and pride,
waiting for rain.

We have felt it all,
sitting on a school bench.

– To high school romances & catfights

R.I.P. GRANDPA

"Only some people LIVE, others just try to stay alive."

The thing that I miss the most
about my Grandpa is the way
he used language like he owned it.

Some essays and letters written by him,
Grandma has still hidden.

I wish to go back to my old town,
to experience his presence in the air.
Catch a glimpse of him,
warming himself up near the furnace,

where Grandma comes close to fuming
his vowels and consonants away,
every single night!
But does not.

I miss the way he described the raging river that
flowed near my summer house.
In his stories and poems, in metaphors
and similes;
He makes them come alive.
Flowing in small streams,
surrounded by long cheddar trees,
and mountain breeze
which makes the leaves sleep.

I miss his lively laugh sometimes.
People laugh around me a lot, I've come to realize.

But no happiness in their eyes, to my surprise.
Only those who live happily die happy.
Wanting to flee to the other world
He rests in peace.

My grandfather is happy where he is!
And I am happy for him,
Though I miss him.

CHOCOLATE BROWNIES

Love tastes like chocolate brownies to me
With walnuts of arguments and
the sweetness of chocolate.
Oh, how it makes me feel!

Adding a scoop of vanilla,
not thinking about my weight.
I let the chocolate brownie consume me.

It has more power over me
than it should.
I would abandon love out of
my everyday diet

if only I could! But I cannot!
Tempting are the love letters,
the chocolate brownie keeps sending!

Only one solution exists:
Doctor Love says to have 'love' in small bits
during breakfast.
The only way how love in my life
can exist.

It can exist, but only in small bits.

– My latest prescription from Doctor Love

SMOKING IS INJURIOUS TO HEALTH.

I want to be that cigarette
that touches your lip
Burns when you breathe;
while holding it with a loose grip.
And ashes out.

What I mean is;
I want you to ruin me.

I want to be the pillow on your bed
Lies still, no words said.

On happy days, and when you're sick
Till your neck, makes my cotton sink.

What I mean is,
I want you to ruin me.

I want to be that cigarette
that touches your lip

Burns when you breathe;
while holding it with a loose grip.
And ashes out.

What I mean is;
I want you to ruin me

WHERE ARE MY WINGS?

I often dream I am falling from a cliff.
A cliff very high. And my wings don't open.
The air doesn't blow, it's dead quiet.
Just a lament. Pin-drop silence.
Where are my wings?

Where are my Wings?

Just moments ago, they were right in my sight.
My strength, my power, and my might.

Where have they vanished?
How will I fly take off from this corrupted land
and dive into the sky?

Where are my Wings?
The light blue vastness of the sky awaits me!
Amongst those fluffy clouds is my home, PARADISE.

Have you seen my wings?
My mother is looking for me!
She's asking my friends-
the stars, the moon and those beautiful birds,
if they have seen her child.

Can you please look for my wings?
I'm starting to cry as it was better if I had died.
For I cannot return home.
Have you seen my wings?
Please be honest! Help me end my exile.

I have lost my wings.
I've been wondering now,
I may never find them.
I am tired.

I used to hope but
this isn't how I was wired.
I have lost my wings, Mum.
I cannot return home.

Mum's note descends from high above,
"You stopped believing, my girl." her words ring clear.

I close my eyes, propelled by faith and love.
Finding solace, banishing my fear,
I take off.

Elated that I have finally found the cure.
I can always grow my wings back, if I will to fly.
I just have to believe.

– Sometimes you just have to believe and things
fall into place.

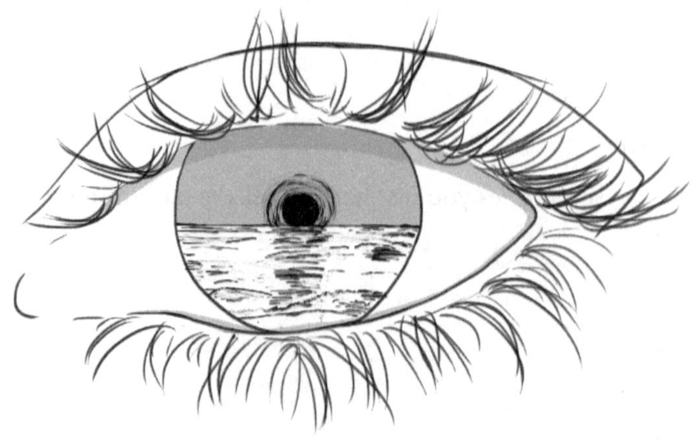

TSUNAMI

The Sea was still.
A calm before the storm.
Your hands were cold;
I swear I didn't know!
A Tsunami at hand;

– Our Relationship

THE MOUNTAINS

"There are two things I love doing more than anything in the world; going to the Mountains and dancing in the rain."

I see the mountains
in the morning's perfect golden light.
Covered trees in the snow,
a river flowing by the side.

An old cottage that smells of
old bourbon and wine.
Pin drop silence
from 7 to 9.

I see the mountains.
I want to climb, another adventure,
till another sunrise.
From dawn to dusk, noon to dinner time.

I see the mountains; it's no crime.
I see the mountains when I close my eyes.
They're my guilty pleasure, my personal paradise.

I see the Mountains when I close my eyes,
sitting in a traffic jam,
in a city of corruption and lies.
I see the mountains; they make me smile.

**– The mountains are always calling and I must most
definitely go.**

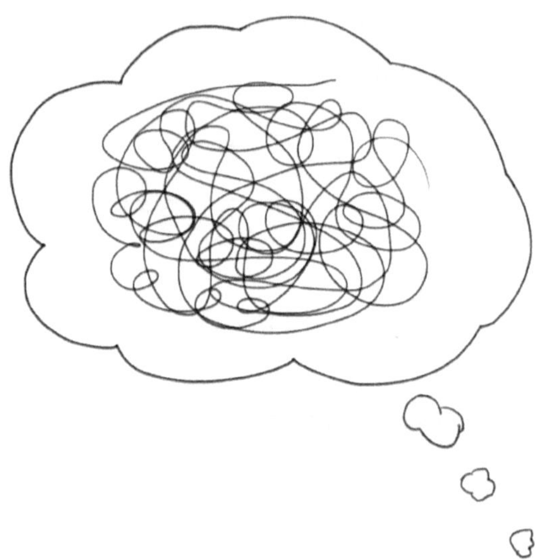

A THOUGHT IN A BOOK

I wish I was a thought in a book,
freshly conceived.
but yet to be written,

I wish I was a thought
the author meant to write.
But couldn't.

I wish I was a thought trapped inside
his chaotic mind and played with other
thoughts that he had.

Maybe there is no reason he didn't write me.
Maybe he didn't get the words right,
or the thought didn't make any sense to him,
later, when he saw it from a distance.

Or maybe he loved the thought too much,
for it to be shared with the world.

Maybe he didn't write me because
writing me off would take everything in him.
And then I would be accessible to everyone.
So, he shut the world out and kept me safe
within his mind only for himself.

– I wish I was a thought in a book yet to be written.

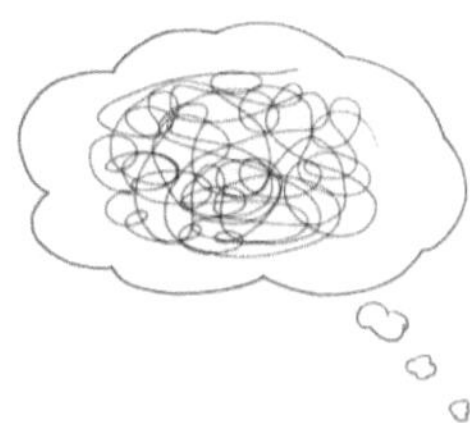

GOLDEN CHILDHOOD

Last night, I fell into an old dream.

So beautiful and simple, everything seemed.

The familiarity of childhood and careless attitude,

not knowing of heartbreak,

pain, or solitude.

The dream was of a random day from my golden time.

Back when I did not know about the world

and would just play day- long with windchimes.

A busy day at my ancestral sweets shop,

eating deserts and dancing around in my pink frock.

Mummy comes to me and kisses me,

as soon as she finds time.

Even though I am a pain in her neck, I know I drive her insane.

The homework, the punishments, mocks, and fights.

The childhood, my childhood drifted away,

and now I'm here in the city of lights.

It's good being right here, but there's a lot that I miss.

I could be a child again. That's all that I really wish.

AUTUMN LEAVES

Like Autumn leaves as the wind blow,
my problems gather and collect on the floor.
Hopeless,
I stand looking at the ground,
instead of finding the escape to the 'Anywhere door'.

My autumn leaves weigh heavily upon me,
wishing to unburden and break free.
To fly with the birds and feed on the trees.
A cyclone comes
and my autumn leaves
swirl around me
and I?

I stand still for I have heard,
when a storm comes
you don't fly away with the birds.
You stand strong and take cover to face the storm.

LET LOVE BE LOVE

Why is love limited to a person, place, or a thing?
Why can't it be something abstract like the breeze,
which touches your cheeks gently?

Why can love not be like a splash of flavour in your mouth?
Like when you have a bite of a mixed iced lolly.
Or a perfume made of the fragrances of Petrichor and
the Night blooming jasmine?
Or the sweet smell of one's homeland?

Why can't love be in moments, and not 'forevers'?

Why is love hated so much? Why can the world just mind its own business? How does 'who you love' matter so much? Why can't love be a personal thing?

If I love, can't I just love? Just be love?

THE ONE

Impure thoughts corrupt
every nerve of my mind,
like a virus, sent to a computer,
Of a fresh kind.

An aftertaste of liquor
and the coarseness in his voice.
The smell of cigarettes,
and his beautiful face by my side.

His eyes, like an ocean,
silent, towards the shore.
His laughter, so infectious,
doesn't let me leave the door.

Arrested by his looks,
captivated by his soul.
Was he the one, I had been waiting for?

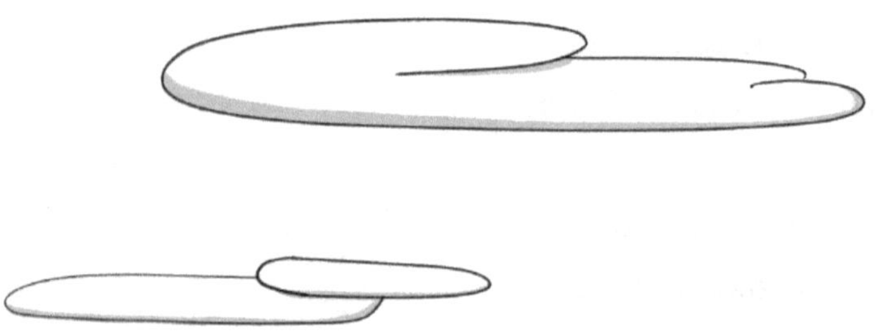

DREAMS UNBOUND

The stillness of the water,
the chaos of the clouds,
the wind in nature's order;
talking to me out loud.

The medium-dark shade
of the green grass separates
me from the crowd,
the buzzing sound helps me meditate,
and the strong-willed mountain birds
coo in the background.

I run bare feet,
my dreams are unbound.
I get lost, to never be found.

LONELY ANCIENT TREE

I am that lonely ancient tree by
the end of the university lake,
quiet and strangely silent.
A place to bring along a date.

I am gigantic and tall.
You should come visit me in the fall,
smelling of damp soil in the rain.

My kids are sweet as sugar cane.
I want to shelter you in an unfortunate time
keep you away from apocalyptic signs.
But I need to feel safe, first, my child.

Setting me up on fire is a trait,
well-known to your kind humankind.

– Save Trees.

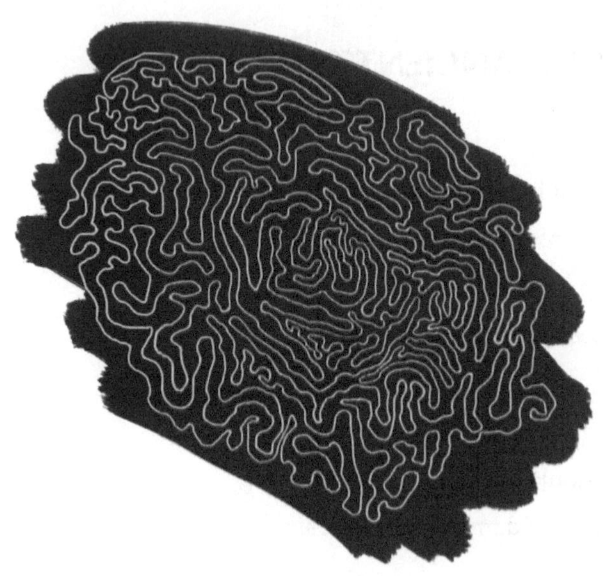

IF YOU WERE A PLACE

If you were a place, you would be cold and coarse.

Barren and empty.

Not even a bark of a dog would be heard.

Pin-drop silence, not a single word.

You'd be like a maze

with a dead end.

A treacherous jungle with

death lurking within.

People wouldn't hear about you
Even if they are even thinking about crossing by your side.
If they do make sure you serve your purpose right,
I say this because I have seen you destroy lives.
I've seen you feed on the misery.

I say this because you're like a serial killer
devoid of niceness.
What happened so wrong babe?
Where did all your love and compassion evade?
If you were a place, I'd call you home.
Even though, I know, you'd drain me out.

If you were a place, I'd try to rebuild you.
The sad part is that you are not a place.
You are a person.

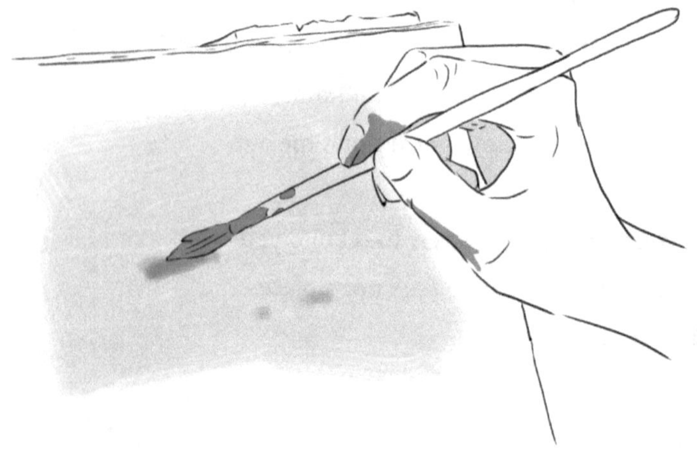

ON HEARTBREAK

Shattered into 1 million pieces, my heart
Crumbled, walked over, and insulted my soul.
Sewing my core, I became art.
True love, my friend, happens but once.

TO FREEDOM

I feel guilty when her skin brushes against mine,
a rush from head to toe, my cheeks shine.
She is everything I wish for.
Trapped in the four walls of my corporate cage,
she is everything I need to
feel awake.

MIXED FRUIT JAM

I cannot keep writing poems
for a love that smelled
like mixed fruit jam
but tasted sour!

I cannot keep giving a damn
and wasting away my precious hours

when his love was a cactus,
instead of a bunch of flowers!

I cannot keep remembering his birthdays
those precious special dates.
And how devilishly handsome
he looked in those shades.

For it pains me to remember it all.
You should rise in love, and not fall.
I tell myself, again and again.

That he cheated- it makes me feel sane.
But he did not!

DON'T YOU WORRY

Sneak into my room and turn on the light.
It'll be dark soon. Don't you bring home any fights.

Sit by me and we'll talk for hours.
Forget the world and those scars.

There isn't any guarantee of life nor there is any to death!
Neither to survival nor to the last breath!

You've gone through a lot
but don't you just go crying- "Why did it not last!"
I know it, baby, even I have been through it all!
Don't you cry-
my baby, my princess, my doll!

Smile sunshine, you have been sad enough lately,
Dance, through life; it has been tough lately.

The night is to fade and it's time for you to shine!
Now it's time for you to shine, my dear sunshine.

No one was ever worth your tears!
Sooner or later you will realize.
Fall for someone over again but this time, just be a little
wise.

– To my sisters with broken hearts

EVERY RAIN...

My mother often sits by the window,
watching the rain.
Writing about some summer love,
which took her heart away.

My mother often sits by the window,
watching the rain.
I look at her smiling sincerely at her notebook.
Am I a part of this vicious chain?

Looking at her,
I feel a little helpless.
I feel maybe,
I will also just keep him
with me
in my writings,
but just the writings.

A doorbell rings and that's all it takes.
She tears up the page in hassle
and throws it away in the bin.
Her love story lies in a corner,
crushed and crumbled.
Dad enters.
Mom stumbles.

I close my eyes and go to my safe space.
my world of dreams, my picture-perfect dreamland.

"Sleep well my baby," she utters in my ear.

A tear rolls down her cheek,
she wipes it away, clear.

– Mothers, wives, friends, sisters.

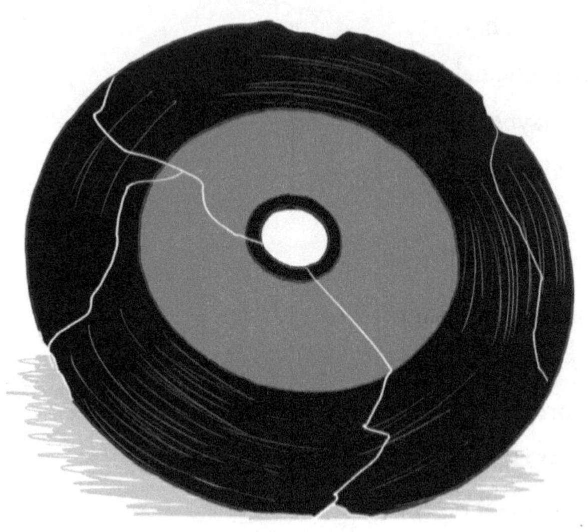

A POEM, HE WAS.

A poem, he was;

beautiful and broken.

A soulful voice;

coarse and cold.

A record put on loop,

or an empty letter.

A paint so sad, no one could

make him feel better.

No one understood him,

His pleasure or his paradise.

No one saw the pain buried
deep within his eyes.
The room would just cheer up
when he would smile.
But when he asked me if I loved him,
I plainly lied.

I bite my tongue
When someone asks me,
"Have you no guy who loves you insane?"
I hesitate at the vowel,
which is the initial of his name.
I swear when I don't see
His face in the crowd.
I just want to call his name out loud.

A poem, he was;
Beautiful and broken.
A soulful voice;
Coarse and cold.

A record put on a loop,
or an empty letter,
A paint so sad,
no one could make him feel better.

WHAT BECAME OF US

He was a volcano,
I was water.
He left, and then
I was all floods and cyclones.

TIME FOR RAIN

Earth yearned for love,
turned barren and dry.
Plants withered, animals starved
and we, humans? Cried.

Angry and hot,
lifeless, it appeared.
Lack of love can do that
to anyone.

A cool breeze brushed Earth's arm,
it flirted with her and teased.
Trees swayed to a symphony,
which it created, with much ease.

Clouds gathered around as a gift,
a raindrop fell to the ground.
Farmers rejoiced- it was time for rain.

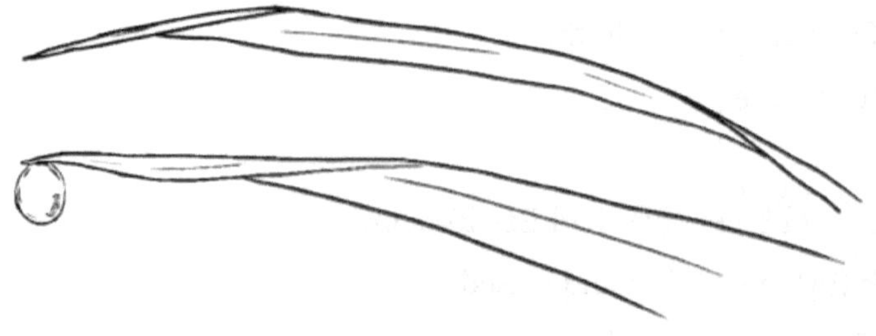

YOU

At first, I thought
you are like water:
going where the path takes you.

Other times I thought,
you are fire:
tough and relentless.
No one could come your way.

But it turns out that you are ice:
seeming to be unbreakable but with a little
warmth, one can make you melt.

ANXIETY

Anxiety doesn't know
how to communicate with me.
It sends signals
to my body.

My hands shiver,
my breath trembles, at times.
Pen gives up,
my mind explodes in what,
where and whys?

**– Anxiety doesn't know how to
communicate with me.**

BROKEN

He was beautiful but broken.
I used gold and filled in the gaps;
gave him my hours, days, and months.

He was perfect again,
for someone else.

Doesn't this happen to the best of us?

– Healers, everywhere.

SCARS AS MEDALS

Somehow, I try to weave poetry into my dress
and carry the scars like medals on my body.
But my trauma pulls me back from behind
and makes love to me, head to toe.
My trauma knows
how to get back at me.
And I can't say no.

MY NAME IS LOVE

My name is Love,
and I hurt!

My name is Love,
and I hurt!
My name is Love
and I am absurd.

My aim: destruction
My strength: your weakness.
My reason for existence: attraction
My reason for extinction: carelessness.

My name is Love,
and I hurt!
My name is Love
and I am absurd.

My name is Love,
but I wasn't meant to hurt!
My name is Love
and it is you people, who make me seem absurd!

GUILTY

I am guilty of the choices I have made.
I hope it is not so late.
I am guilty of the choices I have made.

Endured the abuse, day after day.
I am guilty of not calling out for help,
Did nothing, but just silently hid and wept.

Guilty for I would hide my scars,
under my thighs and beneath my scarf.

Washed away the pain with a façade so bright.
For years, I have carried this burden,
I'm guilty I couldn't put up a fight.

But at the age of 10, who knows the ways of the world?
I was a child, he made me a girl.
Grew up way before my time,
Snatched away my innocence; he wasn't kind.

Mum, filled with fear, tried to keep me locked inside.
"A girl must be protected," her battle cry implied.
Attend school, eat, and study
Don't watch Tv. Like THAT ruined me!

Harm found its way.
Who said, harm cannot come inside?
Home is a four-letter word, but not always 'safe', right?

The abuser was the son of my Uncle's wife.
He stayed in our house,
we played at night.
He would play the groom; and I, the bride.

HER

Smelling of Jasmine flowers, she crossed
me in the office alley again today.
She looked perfect like a painting,
or a melody, that has just been created.

She smiled at me, like she often does
with a certain acknowledgement on her face.
I smiled back, but my eyes were numb.
It had certainly been long enough!

We have shared a long and strong history,
She and I.
One, she will never conform to.
Seeing her again brings back
so many memories-
I swear it's not what you think.

                         – We both have been abused.

STORM WITHIN

I am the rain, falling from the sky;
the heavy downpour that can
wash away all your lies,
and shake you to your core.

I start subtly but go all out,
the way dance progresses;
begins slow but pours and pours,
with thunder and lightning that follows through.

A force of nature, that cannot be denied
I am power, freedom, and I am grace.

I challenge norms, every single day.
Unbound by the chains of society,
I fall where I wish, with no propriety.
I challenge the idea, of being tamed.
For my wild, cannot be named.

So let me fall, and let me roar
For in my drops, lies so much more
A message of hope, for every soul
That we are all equal, and can take control.

– Every girl is a storm within.

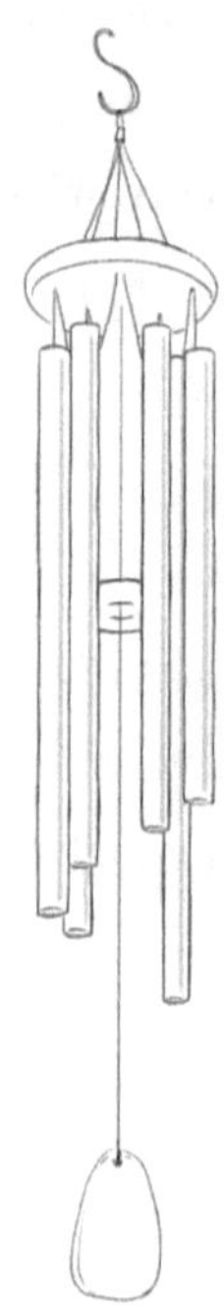

POETRY IS THE AIR SHE BREATHES

Ink splashes upon that blank lonely page,
making love to the emptiness
in her life.

It makes her feel free from her cage
of utter consciousness.

She fathoms creating patterns and lines
with this ink.
Form letters, words, and sentences
in alliteration and repetition.
Rhyme with a reason
and manifest phrases to
dwell in a poem.
Nothing else feels so satisfying
If said otherwise, she'd be lying.

Hidden safely in these pages
are stories unsaid,
emotions undelivered,
concerns unaddressed,
wars unaccounted for,
memories that are sour
and things she will never say.

In verses, she pens down her loneliness
at nights that she can't sleep.

Poetry is the air she breathes
Poetry is the air she breathes.

A JUNGLE SAFARI

Roar of an engine,
shatters the serene.
Innocent creatures,
hiding behind the tall trees.

A jeep, full of idiots,
with guns in their hands.
A hunger too big,
In their cruel hearts.

Throwing light in their homes,
finding excitement in their fright.
Breaking every rule,
they raid into the night.

Disturbed by their presence
a barking deer runs,
across the road with fear in his eyes.
It runs through the woods
for its dear life.

It's fun for them,
the hunt and the chase.
A gunshot fires at last.
The poor chap is dead,

A grand feast in the jungle,
with bonfire and wine.
They celebrate death,
they aren't kind.

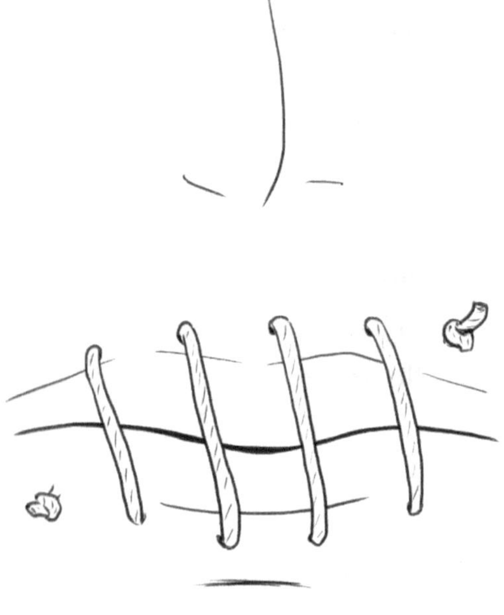

SLEEPLESS NIGHTS

I, often have a dream,

late in the night.

When the world is asleep,

but my mind is running wild.

I dream I am at the top of a tall building,

Or at the top of a cliff;

whatever feels right

I look down,
and someone pushes me.
I fall and fall into an abyss,
My soul transverses like I'm having a fit.

I shout. I scream.
But the words don't
come out.
Someone shushed me again,
For the millionth time!

I wake up from the dream,
and utter a sigh.
'Why that dream again?'
He asks, I don't tell him why!

I express whatever I feel,
In every verse, every line.
Of the things, I write.
I will never be shushed again in my life.

FROM THE PEN OF THE ILLUSTRATOR

Rain is my lover. Every time my heart wails, the rain and wind come to my rescue and put a smile on my face. They fill me with an adrenaline injection that makes me feel that I am seen by the universe, it acknowledges my existence and responds back with kindness, strengthening my will to live on. That being said, to have a friend so close, who shares a similarly intimate relationship with the rain, it was fate that we both got together on this project.

This book holds a lot of memories that are frozen in time and UD's (as I dearly call her) words have dared to make it immortal on these pages. Ever since I have known her, I have always been in awe of UD's sincerity towards her work and that's when she shines the brightest for me. I hope I was able to hold the emotions she wanted to evoke in the readers, through my visuals. I feel my job is well done only when the patron is moved beyond their expectations from the outputs, so I truly hope that you are satisfied with the illustrations UD and not just saying for my sake.

Our process was simple. Partly because I know her well enough to understand where her emotions are coming from and she was clear in her vision as to what she wants from the images. Don't we all love clients like that! Thereafter, I tried to go beyond by trying different perspectives on these images. Each image has been referenced from royalty-free search engines and has my own additions in it. Although I won't be able to pick my favourite artwork out of them, but gun to my head, I would say the treehouse was my favourite one. I was around 5 years old when I made my first tent from grandma's saree, towels, and two chairs. So, the feeling of a safe haven is very comforting for me. My own sanctuary.

Dear readers, the poems and illustrations together are there to add to your personal stories of life and find a sense of shared feeling amongst us. Udbhavi has worked hard for a year to bring this book alive and I got on board in the last 2 months. Regardless of our timeline, our main efforts are towards how these poems reach your heart and tear down some walls that may have been standing tall for a long time. With this, I wish you had a happy reading.

Lots of love!

– **Dipti Ronghe**
(Illustrator)